praise for Reader, I

"Corey Van Landingham makes use of all her imaginau̇.
her lived experience to yield moments of sublimity, humor, sadness,
and joy. And the real gift of this work is Van Landingham's ability to
transform the mundane into that which is sacred through a kind
of plainspokenness that makes the entire text look like magic: 'He
wiped my face. Lingered at my lips to brush a crumb. This was not
my worst, he said. He said it like I could be beautiful again.' *Reader, I*
is a no-holds-barred romp of poetry full of formal innovation and
wonder."

—Jericho Brown, winner of the Pulitzer Prize for *The Tradition*

"Wickedly learned, Corey Van Landingham's *Reader, I* is a tome chock-
full of literary allusion and so terrifyingly clever it offers for serious
readers of poetry intense pleasure. Imagine Shakespeare's sonnet
sequence mated with a stack of bridal magazines. Imagine Dickinson
ghostwriting Martha Stewart. This is territory I've come to think of as
Learned Woman's Hell. It can be difficult here. Smart women know they
risk everything if they commit to a cis-het partnership. We've read the
books. Yet this one is written from the other side. And its achievement is
how far it takes us. The beauty of marriage is in the mundane. It might
even make you, Reader, believe in love. In the Real Thing."

—Cate Marvin, author of *Event Horizon*

"Corey Van Landingham negotiates between an alleged Victorian
decorum and an undeniable contemporary lyricism that dazzles, even
as it holds us close. In one of her central poems, 'The Marriage Plot,' she
writes that 'We were reared // on Wharton and Brontë, on / Waugh . . .
//rooting through our pasts // to find some common / ground.' *Reader, I*
is a marvel of this common ground made of both learnedness and crazy
play, wit and revelation, in poems of tremendous elasticity of design—
from slender, sinuous lines to blocks of epistolary prose that display
Van Landingham's intimacy and her irony. Hers are poems of identity
and cultural bearing, negotiating selfhood within (and without) the

institutions of nation and marriage, citizenship and readership, winking, promising, and enlightening all the way."

—David Baker, author of *Whale Fall*

"'It seemed to me the greatest risk // was to become too legible.' Acerbically humorous and occasionally melancholy, Corey Van Landingham's *Reader, I* examines the absurd conventions of heteronormative marriage. We feel its historic and cultural freight lurking around every corner: a frat party where young women dressed as brides are handcuffed to their 'grooms' for the evening; a speaker struggling with the challenge of trying to piss while wearing a wedding dress; a wedding anniversary at the site of a Civil War battlefield; a catalogue of Lover's Leaps. And yet, this is not a cynical book; Van Landingham faithfully makes space for vulnerability, tenderness, and wonder: 'When we work alone we love each other better.' Reader, be warned: if you've ever navigated the strangeness of being a We, you may very well recognize yourself in these compelling poems."

—Nicky Beer, author of *Real Phonies and Genuine Fakes*

READER, I

COREY VAN LANDINGHAM

SARABANDE BOOKS | LOUISVILLE, KY

FIRST EDITION

Publisher's Cataloging-In-Publication Data
(Provided by Cassidy Cataloguing Services, Inc.).

Names: Van Landingham, Corey.
Title: Reader, I / Corey Van Landingham.
Description: First edition. | Louisville, KY : Sarabande Books, [2024]
Identifiers: ISBN: 978-1-956046-25-0 (paperback) | 978-1-956046-26-7 (ebook)
Subjects: LCSH: Marriage--Poetry. | Married women--Poetry. | Man-woman
relationships--Poetry. | Intimacy (Psychology)--Poetry. | Self--Poetry. | LCGFT:
Domestic poetry.
Classification: LCC: PS3622.A585494 R43 2024 | DDC: 811/.6--dc23

Exterior by Sarah Flood-Baumann.
Interior by Danika Isdahl.

Printed in USA.
This book is printed on acid-free paper.
Sarabande Books is a nonprofit literary organization.

CONTENTS

It is a solemn and strange and perilous
thing for a woman to become a wife.

—Charlotte Brontë, in a letter

Reader, I married him.

—Charlotte Brontë, *Jane Eyre*

READER, I

Reader, I

was, according to Virgil, always a fickle, unstable thing. Woman. *Wyf*. Merger of *wife* and *man*. To indicate: not-girl. Not-yet-claimed, not-yet-weeping. And aren't they often weeping? The mother, tearing her hair out, running toward the battle lines, filling heaven with her womanly wailing. Dido watching those pale, bulging sails leave Carthage. Creusa—first wife—grabbing at Aeneas's ankles as he flees his son, his house? He relents. Allows her to join *at a good interval behind*. And get this—he doesn't look back. Only once he's skirted Troy, left behind the equestrian pyre, the serpents swallowing boys whole, once he's arrived at the mountain gates, only then does Aeneas turn. *Alas*, he goes. He didn't *think to look for her*. Sure, he grieves. Returns to the scalding city before finding her ghost. But never did he turn. This is the forest primeval. The left-behind wives and the wailing, those empires built on our shades. Dactyls upon dactyls of bridal beds aflame, sad wraiths, lustrous oceans of tears. As if woman were a climate, a misdirection of wind. Dock unmoored. Alas. And yes, Aeneas, too, weeps. In the underworld, Dido wandering the Fields of Mourning, and he wants to know—he wants to know if he made her do it, bring her body down, on top of his sword. *Was I the cause?* he asks. He asks her that. This fickle thing. But she's so sturdy here. Look at her. She is granite she is dim moon she is dark grove is sea unchartable. She will not return. She will not return his gaze.

I.

GILLY'S BOWL & GRILLE

As for the beer, I bring my own. I haven't touched
                another human
in twenty-three days, not even someone's palm

                passing my change.
I forget—because I am in heels, because the West
                still owns

a portion of my body, and is on fire—my socks.
                The owner
of the alley lends me his daughter's,

                who is behind
the concession counter and looks, in braces,
                blond hair

twisted on top of her head, like she could
                be mine. *They're clean*,
he tells me. Crew, bleached white, mid-Atlantic

                preteen packaged.
She wants, I am sure of it, something synthetic.
                She wants,

in pink polka dots, in patterned tiny stereos,
                to forget
the same five boys corralling the boxes of M&Ms,

                sodas sweating
in their Styrofoam cups. Peeling out on the simulated
                driving games,

they push in quarter after quarter she drops to their
                     cupped hands.
And as I test each polished orb for weight, I think

                  the white, ribbed
cotton socks are the rows of corn she rides
                  her brother's bike

by. Shoot after shoot of the alleys
                  she sweeps
after the boys are picked up and taken home.

                  I drink
the beer her father wouldn't, brewed in a fancy
                  coastal town.

I'm not, we both know, from around here. No one else
                  bowls alone.
I christen each column with a name I always wanted.

                  Brooke. Madison.
Biblical *Joannas*, *Rachels*, *Lydias*. Women with history.
                  The children

I will never have. The year my father died
                  I swore it—
never leave another behind. Keep to yourself.

                  Move often,
and far, and spend your money. It is, I hope,
                  his business—

Gilly's—named for her, so that, when she has moved
                  to Pittsburgh,
or Cleveland, and he has been gone almost half her life,

        she can know
he wanted, for her, somewhere that people would drive to,
          in the dark,

to drink under the neon lights and hurl their lives away
          for an hour
or two. To sweat into her own socks, which will still

        be here—
clean, white, and when they place them
         on the counter,

a man might grab a stranger's hand
        and tell her
she cannot leave with her open bottle of beer.

Reader, I

did take a walk that day. In the park, prefair, rides in their peeling cages. Yet to unfurl their ribboned neon across the dark. Dust glittering in May's godlight. I did not say I would be his chariot (perhaps its battled rust). He did not proclaim himself viceroy of unfettered happiness (there was nothing so grand for us). We knew the sheer cliff of augury. Of contract. Of futures compounding in our joint portfolio. We passed the coin-mucked pond, the Bud truck with its capillaries of beer untapped. Swings lonely for children. Lotto tabs still unpulled. Gentle reader, in some savage country of summer, the corroded Comet would, late-season, like an angry god throw a man through the sky. I did not tell him there would be no pain. That love would make us free. It was only spring. Vetch hasped against the chain-link fence. A robin delivered its largo to the weeds. Who, though, doesn't imagine that flung moment? Pendulum ablaze. You can view it (really) in a video. We pressed pause, rewind. Then play.

Reader, I

swore I'd be a casual bride. The dress code nonexistent (I shan't have lied), beer in cans. I wanted, only, a single gerbera daisy placed in each glass bottle. Red. Just that. I only browsed the magazines to roll my eyes. *Martha Stewart, Southern Bride.* The gloss too slick, affairs too rich to find myself inside. We scoffed at rowboats all beflowered, the ceremonies lit by tiki torch under Bora Bora skies. Engraved soles—*I do*—pressed against the ballroom floor received light snickers, snide retorts. Cake toppers, real hair! We would never . . . Leather Dopp kits for the groomsmen, monogrammed panties for the girls. The condo-priced gown . . . just a moment of weakness. I gave it a try. A smart-skirted woman advised a garment to mellow out my thighs. It did. Though under all that tulle they could already hide. Just a touch of rouge, some glue to tack the extra lashes on my eyes. Did they have a shade of lipstick to match my groom's tie? One named for a city we both admired? *Toledo*, perhaps? *Telluride*? The makeup counter had a gleam I liked. There were tubes of cream for every divot over which I cried. I sat long nights under the kitchen lamp trying to decide: Which skin type was my own? Combination, dry? Shall I bleach my asshole? Offer guests a fan, insecticide? Was I an Elizabeth Taylor or a Scarlett, hair untied, would he prefer lingerie with lace? A dewy or a matte face? Would his father's tux prove excessive for the lakeside wedding? My mother's jewels? Should we move the reception to a gallery, no distracting view? Where the bridesmaids' spray-on makeup wouldn't melt, where I could remove my shoes to glide for a moment or two under the French horn's simple song—just a rustic tune—unadorned. Is it too late to book a riverboat—imagine!—for July? Fireworks as we say goodbye? I fear I'm botching the script; please advise.

Mamma V's Basement Lounge

Questi, che mai da me non fia diviso

We have never been so young.
Its cement floors keep the patrons—coeds
mostly, shirking finals prep—cool.
No windows. The young men are a kind,
I say, I've never wanted. Khakied, polo shirts
pressed, prepped for a future
of futures and real estate. The women
though. They are—in white
summer dresses, eyelet lace, ruffled
trim, or backless, polyester
stretching across their chests—like
a dream. Or a video I, too, have watched
in winter's lonelier months.
They are dressed as brides.
A student explains this, in line
for another round of discounted
vodka drinks, for we,
their teachers, are barred
from these rituals, this
fine-tuned debauchery.
For an evening (invisible SigEp
decree) the women come
with their flower crowns and ivory
frocks. Then they are handcuffed—small,
uncomfortable laugh—
to their grooms. Mild protesting.
Shy looking back. They perform
their duties. In the musty frat house
a new bride undoes

with her one free hand
the neat bow at her nape, cleans,
we're told, some piled
dishes, scrubs on her knees
the grimy tile. This
is what they think of marriage.
In a matter of months, we
will be wed on the long, solemn staircase
leading to a part of the school
they will never visit, the Office
for Sad Reaching Out
to Past Students for Just
a Small Donation. But here,
now, the dream-girls descend.
They gather in the basement bar, tied
to the men buying them
too-sweet shots. Dante knew this hell—
haunted Francesca with Paolo's shadow,
chained sodomites to each other
in threes. Suicides forever
fed-on by a harpy's insatiable
beak. Strapped together in swamps
and dark chutes, the dance floor
so packed their sweat
is the sweat of one. They do not know
the stink and rot that flesh
becomes. But who, having memorized
how it all ends—four galloping
horsemen, constant rain of fire, moon
like blood—wouldn't still choose
this? One evening of panting
into each other's ears?
Distracted beauties and their attendants
crowd the bar like they deserve—
they *do*—the bartender's favor.

We will remember them like this.
By midnight the flowers in their hair
begin to wilt. Handcuffs flashing
under the disco ball's brief light. Who was ever
so young? We must leave them,
return to our nightly routine
of stated love before we switch off
the lamp. We who will be bound
together by law, who have chosen
a forever unimaginable
to the couples still pressing
against each other in the dark bar's
pulse and stench. We who would forgo
all that. We have imagined
the ache and sag. The last
words. Collapsing
into bed, we agree there is nothing
for us out there.

Reader, I

wore the past around my neck like a pendant. There were empty metal chairs for the men no longer with us and for once euphemism seemed a good cloak. Our vows were Roman. The color of my dress *Antique*. Diamonds from a great-aunt I never knew—sapphires, blue. No, I wore nothing at my throat. Except a belief that two syllables could save us. We were deepening. We stepped out of the designated day—flies hovering over our banquet of hot dogs, oiled chips—like stepping from a cooling bath. We emerged so into myth. Skipped ahead to the eternal. I swear, that's how we illuminated ourselves. We wrote each other letters. Quoted Milton. That cavalier. Discarded our separate tragedies for one. The uncertain world before us. Sparta even, for the good ten years. Then I left my bouquet of thistles on the trolley. The frosting melted at a brief summer rain. Sad, molecular, a punch shifted in its cut crystal. We pictured, already, our children picturing us when we're dust. Plato: *The desire and pursuit of the whole is called love*. So we surrendered to happiness. Last in our rented hall, I thought we might survive it. We pulled down the stringed lights. He held my dress's heavy beading above my head and recited a poem about Ohio—about sure decline, and how what's beautiful can kill us—while I peed.

Reader, I

studied sonnets on a chaise longue in Charleston. Each small
song clarified the couplet, the fevered rhetoric of two held
together, in the rental car, on the long drive south. Each day
we were more married, more varied in how we touched. It once
made me sad. That much would be lost, and soon—*Nothing but
tenderness and pleasure*, Samuel Johnson defined that first honeyed
month against the waning moon. On time, Shakespeare alacked
its *wrackful siege*. But dawn's novel idiom arose brilliant from
the harbor. Highballs kept, somehow, the thinnest rime. We
shuttered the hotel windows, plotted years of humid mornings,
scones crumbling in our sheets. What else, reader, could we
script on the Chevy's rear glass? What would seem just still,
returning, as we must, to the year, what would thrill him, might
remind that even a slim crescent dazzles the black ink of night?

American Foursquare

Self-assembled, sure, though the idea at first
was carbon filament and craftsman guilds, one master

sanding the hardwood wainscot. Then the West
unfolding like tapestry toward Klondike.

On a cobblestone block, before our mothers'
mothers' mothers breathed, a home like this

could be mail-ordered, from Sears, from a fabled
city they would never see—four new rooms

in a boxcar shuttling through the switchgrass.
No florid corbelling, no finials.

No caliginous Victorian nooks. No matter
the original flooring sagged

beneath our bookshelves. Midnights
our two-step made the mantle quake. We said yes

to the modest Prairie Box, floorplan
recalling the glacier's carved swath. To structure

married to the ground as Wright proposed, new beds
stretching their savage geometry

to Kearney, Sweetwater. Sometimes
even beauty needs a border.

Only in plowless tracts along the rail cut
does the wild iris cast, still,

its explicit spell. Yes, we believed
in this mythos. We lived between Church

and University, could almost imagine no one
had died there. We hosed the spiders out.

We spent a year of savings on a mission
sofa, an expandable ladder

to reach the dormer's moldered siding. Perma-White
paint. Shirtless, thrown brilliant

bronze, he gripped the brush between his teeth.
History, the point being, requires the most audacious

of lacquers. We wanted natural light, to be hung
in picture windows. Let the neighbors watch

our weekday reverse cowgirl (all the world's
a stage on the corner lot). Each night

our streetlamp, too, turning on
like a new thought.

Reader, I

fled him like an hind. Along the river's sloping edge, the trailbed damp beneath my Nikes. How he relished the hunt, asked, again, if we could do it. *Sic cerva leonem*, naughty boy. I was always granted a head start, substantial (oh, he was fast). So the part of our run where we'd be heading home, I was alone. Sole heart thrashing its chest in the forest clearing. My ponytail swishing like the tail of a doe. I had been living unimagined, undreamed, but here I was mythic beast. Some scene from Grecian vases, my legs shapely against the shallow kylix. Apollodoros, painting in the red-figure period, could finally make the muscles pulse. My dimpled thighs. His gold-struck hair. (What clay could never capture: that finest crevice between threat and play. The sound of his hot breath when the path was too narrow to turn. What uncoiled when he finally touched my sweat-slick neck.) Every match must, eventually, exhaust its limits. This game had boundaries, had rules, but we could wild within it.

Reader, I

buried him. I dug and dug and dug while, across the kitchen island, he—
still smug—crunched the Cheetos. Crunch. Crunch. For this, Venetian
women lost their sight to lace? For the temper's pilot light? No fight that
I could win? (At what point, reader, does a hairline become the break?)
My hands bloodied under a polished moon (I ditched the shovel for
the hysterical spoon and meted out his deepening spot). His marriage
plot. No makeup sex to lick the rift. That I were a woman who could
flick the glassware one by one from the porch . . . My problem, good
reader, is the constant rewind, the projector flashing always against
the tall silo of my mind what he did and didn't. "Were you glad?" the
therapist asked when I replayed the heart attack, the dream, again, of
letting him turn blue on twin petites. I pictured long days scrubbed of
the nothing much that we had said. Impromptu flights to Biarritz. A
rotating fleet of duller men I could pity and kiss. Could you repeat the
question? What *was* it? I could never say exact enough. It was more the
way he said it, yesterday, as if I were a child. The way he proclaimed,
again, perhaps we *weren't* a very good match. Wild, how I could catch
him in a lie (whose number is this?), how his eyes would flash before
he cracked his screen. I swore again and again to leave. I washed my
hands of sod at the side yard spigot. I'd been beguiled. The worried
neighbor pointed at a caterpillar in the carport, its smaller band of
rust. "Trust me." This winter, she said, will not be short, or mild.

ENTR'ACTE

Her Thoughts on the Hereafter

Thinis, Egypt

I talked too much.

It was often remarked, *Amunet, you have too many words.*

True, I would often point out the scorpion ascending the date palm, the man with the face of a donkey. True, I doled out jokes for the servants as they rubbed almond oil into my scalp.

If I stayed outside too long, talking with his tutor, letting my dog run around me, he would pinch my arm and say, *Amunet, do you wish to appear the wife of a swineherd?*

For refuge, my husband hunted ostrich, gone in the desert long days.

He came back with tales of wild cattle, lions that circled his tent at night. How he woke to their cratered paw prints, one less horse.

Hence, the hound.

Menhet, he named her, after the Slaughterer. But she refused to stalk the wild cattle, recoiled from the ostrich's sharp beak. She would whine and whine and whine, *like you*, he said, so like got like—my new friend.

While he was away we would walk the gardens, Menhet and I, accompanied, some mornings, by the tutor, who lectured on history and botany, pointing out the saltcedar, acacia, the pink-flowering willows.

He told me how Hor-Aha was entombed with women, dwarves, even dogs! That they fed his servants poison—to assist the pharaoh, after.

Artists visited our palace to engrave my husband's likeness. They'd position us closer, closer on the siltstone, for eternity.

Not one image of me alone.

I was named, anyway, after the-invisible-one—silent-winged, asp-headed.

How often he would repeat my name, as if to call me back to it, to crawl inside that quiet. *Amunet, Amunet.*

And I feared it, the soul a living thing, that it could so quickly flee me, then pour back in. What if it, too, didn't want me? What if I went flapping along without it, into that next life?

We, like Egypt, would last forever, the tutor told me.

I see that he was mostly right.

I've seen a whole people wiped out by a great wave one thousand years after my death.

A king in France takes a pinch of me, 1524, each morning with rhubarb, so that his enemies will not capture him.

I found nothing bad about you, one husband penned into his wife's coffin.

My mother-in-law, blind for seven years, told me, day of our wedding, *Amunet, you are no great beauty*.

I was lucky, I had been told. The wives of pharaohs have it worse.

They said my soul would follow me here, but I'm somehow smaller. My heart lighter than an ostrich feather. My ankles are so thin.

Centuries of silence. My husband beside me in this clay room.

They said we'd come back to this world with all our treasures, but where's my little dog?

II.

Reader, I

see it first from the window. Body break-dancing around itself. A rabbit's
epileptic fit. Poor pinwheel. Poor whip. The in-between becomes more
brutal. The will-it. The won't. The *don't-keep-watching*, then it's dark.
"Shouldn't we?" I ask, knowing how that *we* falls apart. He catalogues
the possible weapons. The shovel. The brick. The bat we keep in case.
It hurts to look directly at his face, so we both keep watching the grass.
He's gentler than I. Finds no pleasure in pain. Suddenly it sprints—we
go hopeful, silent. Search the night. "There!" Midleap the muscles grab
it back, how it shakes and shakes. We haven't left the kitchen light. I've
read (*Watership Down?*) how they can shriek. What makes us train the
hurt back on ourselves? Why do we stand so touchless? I'm ready to do it,
almost greedy to be good. Check his face for the OK. Turning away, I lose
it. Which should be a happy loss. Which should grant us both good sleep.

Reader, I

was not, I learned, *dis*interested, but *un*-. The bar slowed. Just, honey, so you don't embarrass yourself. (He knows how he sounds.) And I suppose he *was* nonplussed by my usage (I thought: unimpressed). The blank brick walls weren't artless. You've guessed, I'm sure: he's *smart*. His favorite party game: All American Literature Is About . . . while I, the rube, was sucking beer from a plastic tube. And I've been getting dénouement wrong my whole life! All those classrooms I stood before, like *Now we're finally tiptoeing up to The Cow Meant.* Good god. I mean, I've never liked the French (those rude boys at the hostel and their forced kisses, their bossy stench). I guess I'd never heard it said. Confused doff with don (he wanted me to put my bra *on*?). Thought I could see through opaque. Those uneasy chuckles when, last year in my exams, I proclaimed Southey like a Confederate. Language, I tell my students, is prayer, is yoke. A fun house mirror. All my foibles, my thick, flawed patois. One hoppy beer ignites my slur. But I taught him the root of enervate (to cut the sinews of, or weaken—it's not what I thought). How to rim, with an orange skin, the perfect Negroni. All American Literature Is About: the Donner Party (my one flash of brilliance in front of his Berkeley friends). Dear, dear reader—please excuse my flickers of ire. I do admire his brain, the ease with which he speaks. I *like* when he compares my ass to a Man Ray, recites a passage straight from Proust. I just tend to quote, more often, Phoebe Buffay. And now I know: a gathering of apes (our date to the Cincinnati zoo) is actually a shrewdness. (The joke: think a group of wives.) But I'd call that an enervation. You?

Reader, I

have not so much time for thinking. September, 1854. Brontë three months in. Time gone to the needlework, stray visits. Time to the dustpan and the broth. The cough. The pleasant walks. Happy, she still kept stock. That trick about preventing blisters—I fill a plastic bag with water, place it inside my shoe. In the freezer, the leather expands, new form. Thinking—if you'd call it that. My nights more hunting down the danger-lines, the wiry what-ifs. "Calm your mind," he coaxes. As if. Still, there's less room for it—the high beam, the proficient angst. Perhaps a weighted blanket. Something soothing, crochet. All the doctors, all the pills, a journal by the bed. "Are you thinking about what you read?" Thinking. No. Prism in which one Me forgets to say please. One waking with scuffed knees, too many gimlets. Me sitting silent in the room where Father died. Me always-sorry plus never-quite. Me an unphotogenic bride. Me wiving, me future-wide. Me vs. children, my pride. A mirror flashes back your blind spots. A man reveals worse: your possible selves. The you you might have been. See it fill his eyes.

Reader, I

drank the milk of paradise. It made me sick. Wandering the new rooms at night, red rash along the torso. He was North, un-afflicted. I applied a chilly bottle of wine, slept on the hardwood. Who planted the magnolia so close to the house? *Acuminata.* Cucumbertree, fleshy fruit. Which settlers, 1788, midsummer along the glaciated territory, collected. Stored in thick jars of whiskey. One glass, one bitter glass. Who watched the rose-colored wand soften, turn? Take the liquor—autumnal fever prefers a soberer host. It commences with shivering. Cold feet. Just when you think summer has fled you, the leaves split open. Scarlet seeds hang from threads like jewels. Larger than fingernails, than horse pills. Manifold bloodteeth, a ring around the house. I resembled, that month, a parasite—singular, capable of worse. When he returned, he helped me sweep, each thick morning, the fruit from the porch. He drew me baths heaped with colloidal dispersions. Still I itched. Still, in bed, he started with the touch of an icy toe. One glass, one glass. Night-small creatures ran up and down the trunk, so close I could feel the protein in their claws. Take the liquor. Each morning the porch was full, radiant, no matter how much we swept, with rot.

Reader, I

switched to store brand. To cardboard chips, uneven dusting of spice.
("Wouldn't it be nice, to pay down the Visa?") To *facial tissue* and single-
ply, cereals forced to depict *themselves*—no grinning mammal, only skies
of corn, fields of blank plastic. The logs of cheddar only sharp, no Blue
Stilton stinking sweetly in its wax. Unhappy eggs (white, Styrofoam
box). No Halloween pumpkin (it'll only rot). Reader, I felt less . . .
me, sans indulgence. He turned the heat to 63. I froze. I browsed the
rows of luxurious face creams to fix my frown lines, my folded crown.
Bought none. And when he was away? I ate spiteful pho—steaming,
heat he couldn't take—on lunch breaks. Extra tofu, he'd never know.
The nice pinot, too. Brûléed banana ice cream. Orchid face masks, eggs
with golden yolks that almost pulsed. I know, I know—boo hoo. Poor
me, scaling back. All we contain, consume. Divinity isn't only a light
confection. But he buys the entire bar Budweiser after a win. Pays for
Club Seats, season opener, jars of glistening hair pomade. True, I've
become efficient. Ask for the receipt. Eat less meat and add water to
shampoo. You recite weekly mantras too, don't you? (I do not need
quince jam, I do not need the Riesling Kabinett, those purple carrots,
heirloom tomatoes' perfect-dawning skin). We've hoarded a pretty
sum, and I haven't asked my mother for a dime in years. I do not need.
Though—I admit—I spend nights staring at pink armchairs on my
Pinterest page, plan trips to Assisi we'll never take. Alone, my debts
would never be forgiven. I carry with me too much want to live in.

Reader, I

am not so hollow-boned as to suggest a natural bent to flight. But. Caroming down the country road to a motel where the desk clerk, the dandruffed one with ember eyes, knows my face? Dear reader—five times this year I've fled. *Eyre* said men are hard-hearted and I underlined it twice. Five times I've snatched the keys, wobbled into the lobby to sleep on detergent-crusted sheets. Good Grief, I name the place. Hysterical Heart Hotel. I just feel so *much*, sometimes, midaltercation, sound so tin-struck in my whine, believe I might really levitate—such a kingdom is my ire. Jealous Jane Suites. Knights of the Cruel Tongue Inn. Lowing with daybreak, the cows stare through the glass door, through me. Me, I'm morning-sorry. Nothing feels as poker-hot, as gnashing, waking up alone. On the way home the hills are finally tea green, emerging from the mist. Please, I say. Quit turning away. Red-eyed, I explain the busted rearview mirror. Sorry for the Impala, the lofted bottle of vermouth. The underworld of sadness. Understand, reader, that to some women *harbor* means point of departure—cold, stone-walled bay. Vino, veritas. We revolve around future absence. Exactly. You only know the plum is bitter when you've sunk your teeth into its skin. Zeus wielded the thunderbolt; cow-eyed Hera stayed home.

Reader, I

may have been too flip regarding our battlefield wedding   ours
a lesser union   then I heard Benatar in every waiting room
on the rental's radio driving to our honeymoon   the South Beach
karaoke bar   we laughed it harmless   (heartache to heartache)
with some success   on the grand staircase where we wed men from
each side lost their limbs   classes restarted two months later   the
chemistry books were full of actual blood   we fed our guests cupcakes
yes you could say we invited some manner of carnage   I asked my
mother a year later   is this what it's supposed to be like   what's
this   she asked   what's *it*   (we are young)   our apologies were
skipped stones   a winter made us hard and presented the habit
of silence   my necklaces knotted in the move   I was advised how
to work them loose   go back to where it started   we returned for
an anniversary   a small white farmhouse on the military park   we
had not learned from our romance how to separate histories   one
bedroom   few windows   at night the walls seemed to sprout small
beetles   we found them on our pillows each morning   crawling up
through the shower in the distance there was cannon fire from more
lively reenactments   a park ranger told us how the deer were so
small that year   they would startle him as he took his tractor through
the fields   leaping through the tall grass   he took such care not to
nick them   but they could be anywhere you know like the black snakes
hacked by the mower's blades   the finite stop of the box turtle   our
postcards were full of Melville   one evening the house was so full of
us I had to leave   the fireflies so numerous I gasped   it had been
weeks since I was out past dark   reader would you believe I didn't
search the world for metaphors   horse-drawn carriages passed
our door all week desperate for us to wave back   I refused   such
a stubborn ghost   it was hard not to touch each other walking
through the tight rooms   but we had practiced not touching for
some time (heartache to heartache)   one small leather journal told

the house's history   how the farm was ravaged   powder marks
inside the kitchen   two soldiers found underneath the porch
in his orchard four dead Confederates huddled around a cooking
pan   every fence post gone missing   plus two cows   one
calf   his cobbler's tools   his leathers   in September his daughter
died   imagine   this is where we slept   in adjacent twin beds
weeks after the battle that farmer looked out and saw one cow
and her calf returned   imagine   the ground still mostly blood
and shit   his damage claims denied   one brilliant white cow
ambling through the peach orchard   one calf's gummy eyes
(we are strong)   after dinner I would look out the bedroom's
one window   fencerows rebuilt   barn swallows diving through
such slender holes in the wood   (we stand)   I never hold
enough faith   not even for these smallest of resurrections

Reader, I

consider the octopus who flaunts her pink-blushed breadth, webs herself thin, flirts amorphous for the camera before settling inside a clear jar. It shouldn't—I know this—take a man, but waking at dawn, strict hours, hard work—the scissors glint less when you aren't staring them down by moonlight. Less time floating alone in the pity bath. There is an order he brings. Clean lines. Paired socks. No one should expect a marriage to save her. No one should assume she can open the jar herself.

Reader, I

remember the midnights. The hour's stark cleaver—new year from old.
A stranger's clove-tinged mouth, that kindling. Now I'm sleeping on the
couch. We haven't kissed for a week (some winter bug I shouldn't spread)
but I've resolved less pity, less sorrow. Remember, reader, how one glance
could burn right through each scarved layer, touch bone? Tomorrows
upon tomorrows. Embossed bralettes. The rough knuckle tracing a
hipbone while you sidesaddled the chilly fence? Enough—it's untidy,
trawling youth like this. So what if I watch our neighbor step into her
gleaming dress after we kill the lights. We had a glass of wine. There are
branches of eucalyptus inside a glass vase and my husband is dreaming
his same dreams. The years are carbon paper. Jubilee—who could say it
with a straight face? Have we inherited a right to happiness? The leather
cools my fevered cheek, and I'll spare him. We aren't made to last forever.

III.

The Marriage Plot

We can't behave like people in novels, though, can we?
                                          —Edith Wharton

Though, if—

     I might say he was quite
the eighteenth century. *En règle*, decorous in daily
     bow ties. Flashing wit.

That pleasurable pain

     of waking at dawn
to scrub, again, the gutters. His prized
     laser level in the annual

Righting of the Frames.

     Myself—more drinking, more
ninetheenth. Long-winded, a little
     dull in my vast catalogue of woe.

Thoroughly

     bourgeois. I mean, sherry muddied
in a crystal decanter. What can you
     expect? We knew each other first

in a canopy bed,

     in a close room
in an amber state of light,
     still thrilled by the subjunctive.

It was important that we *oxidize*,

      not *age*. Seduced
by private fantasies, I passed out, one evening,
        in grandmother's furs

reeking, still, of smoke.

       *

It seemed to me the greatest risk

      was to become too legible.
Can I say I was a pauper of love? A long moor
        of sorrow? I am not coy

nor slight.

      The best image for which
I strove was *equine*. Regal.
        Sturdy. My main mistake, I found,

in the new era—

      how easily I turned
plinth and pedestal. Bovine.
       My habitual mood

of humiliation,

      self-doubt, forlorn depression,
fell damp on the embers of my decaying ire—
        Unpacking, again,

his heavy books.

*

We were reared

     on Wharton and Brontë, on
Waugh, we found,
       one afternoon,

rooting through our pasts

     to find some common
ground. Whited
       out, aspirational toward

the brooch-filled life.

     Something that should
have rotted centuries ago still
       writhing within us.

We knew what hid

     behind marble fountains,
box seats for *Faust*,
       what lingered in our entwined,

fictional foundations.

     *

We can fall for the pathos

     of the orphan, for the minor
catastrophes of the dashing rake,
       the governess at the country estate

writing epistles

     amongst the saxifrage of Sussex.
We can avoid the advances
     at the Summer House,

delay a little longer

     the central event. We can
take it slow, page by page, count
     the dowagers and deathbeds,

waistcoats and hearths.

     Our gentleness waning,
we can smash a glass or two
     on a Tuesday, unwind some

old wound.

       *

One discovers,

     in the purchase
of shared property,
     other histories over which

one lies.

     The house we bought
vacant for a decade, used for storage—
     an entire room of coats!—

after a local darling's

long courtship with a man
a block away was signed legitimate
by the state.

No children

to divvy up the chinoiserie armoire,
the Wedgwood dinner set
with scenic takes of Yale,

the baby grand,

the neighbors pored over
their worldly, posthumous possessions
in a trio of estate sales.

The realtor staged

a small back room
above the ancient trees as nursery.
Bile green. Which would become

my office.

Which would remind him,
each time he entered
with a cooling cup of tea

how I inherited

not only a handmade Oriental rug
and a caviar spoon carved
from mother of pearl, but

a selfishness

that manifested mostly
in contraction. Who will take
all we'll leave behind, all our

little things?

                    *

On the Romantic Danube

            river cruise my mother booked
for us a month before
            my wedding, I watched her dance

with a stranger

            to a halting "Blue Moon"
broadcast live to our stateroom.
            The sunset

having annulled itself

            hours before, somewhere between
Krems and Vienna, it seemed
            we were floating in deep, dark space.

From my single bed

            I saw her turn
her face from his to laugh, shyly,
            at his request for another song.

She left to refresh her drink

and, in this private showing,
this sitcom spinoff of
        My Life, I tried to conjure

a scene that never was—

        a waltz, a fox trot, some slow
swaying between parents
        in a dimming room.

The closest I got

        (here she returns
to the silver-haired man, here
        they clink highballs

and he takes her hand

        while the pianist limps
into another obvious tune)
        was her catching my father

as he fell

        from the hospital cot
in our living room. How she scooped
        him up under the armpits

in an effortful embrace,

        spinning him
toward the bathroom, where she cleaned him,
        before hoisting him back

where he stopped living.

*

We can imagine ourselves

      an American epic, Copland
booming at sunrise after a battle in which
      we were especially savage.

Like a new nation

      we can discard shame.
We can walk to the grass tennis courts and wave,
      in a summer storm,

our rackets.

      As if to tempt
lightning, or as if we
      were beating out the moths

from exotic carpets

      in a long novel
that half the population
      doesn't have the window-light

to read.

IV.

Lover's Leap

My mother sang the tragedy
          with gusto, summers at the river's
pebbled shore, a rare glassy section beaming back
          the cliff. She did a mean
Johnny Preston, diving deep
          into her Carolina twang, sweet tea
balladeer. Running Bear, it went, loved
          Little White Dove, and you pretty much know
the rest. Separate tribes. Different
          banks. Raging river. Moonlight, quickened
heartbeat, etc. Love that lasts—
          our greatest myth—for always. Forever
together in that happy hunting ground. I mean
          they jumped. In Hawks Nest,
West Virginia, it's Little Swan, Running Deer.
          Big Otter and Laughing Water
plummeting hand in hand in Missouri.
          Twain counted fifty Lover's Leaps
on the Mississippi alone. Fifty indigenous
          brides. Fifty summits.
Fifty faithful plunges toward an eternity in the sky.
          It was, surely, some American
breed of romanticism launching youth
          so fanatically off the edge.
Butch Cassidy and the Kid throwing themselves
          to the swollen river canyon. Huck and Jim
stepping hand in hand toward the raft,
          the future the West
was made of. Off Highway 120. Lake Tahoe.
          Off Bucks Lake Road, California falling
from its golden bluffs. But also,

in Jamaica, on the plantation
east of Treasure Beach, two enslaved lovers legend binds
            together. In Croatia. Bristol. In Brazil. In the emerald
hills of Kodaikanal. Do I believe there is a space
            love crosses? That we accept this death grip?
O, bid me leap—The stories, though,
            built for tourism. Pamphlet narratives,
Sunday drives. Seven states
            visible from the eponymous lookout,
the diner below. Climbers at rest
            with their clips and chalk in the duct-taped
vinyl booths. What business. What myth
            makes a place sweet with.
My mother doesn't actually believe
            in such great woe, drove herself
across the country from a marriage, from Maryland
            to South Dakota, camping
roadside, catching trout, and years
            after my father's death she is still
sitting on a plastic bucket, in the garage,
            singing to herself as she guts a fish for me.

Reader, I

kept my name. No fastening. So I could not become shred. Wing from socket on the highway's sad shoulder. There was some dark pool in the idea—to return to it, after. A shorn beast wearing the coat of its own fur. I preferred how it was duchess, was the riverside enceinte guarding Ghent. The final link to my father, his voice dimmed by the living. Their surging sounds. All it will take, to be alone in it—the death of one uncle for whom I have no great care. Then, each mounting syllable, mine. Then the roomy carriage of it. The box seat empty. Mine, the reins. Is this how Mary feels, sitting alone in her oil panel? Altarpiece wings open. *She is more beautiful than the sun and the army of the stars*, the inscription offers, atop her arched throne. She is *a spotless mirror of God*. But she's more exquisite, gown midnight blue. Mary reads. The light is outside the frame. Mary reads and deep is her concentration, deep is her stare. Lips parted. Gold-flowered corona. Next to her—center panel—the Almighty. But her eyes are elsewhere. Not on his vestments, regal as they are. Not on the silk brocade, its vines and pelicans. Which, reader, spill blood from their own breasts to feed their young. Or so early believers believed. When we threw my father's ashes to the clear river, small fish rushed to the surface and fed. Then he was many. A name is no poultice. Like a Gothic husband— stone-carved, hands folded at his chest—with me alone it will expire.

Reader, I

made my mother cry. Basement of the Italian café, candles cascading over themselves with wax. A wan Chianti to celebrate thirty-three. We had always shared our plates (had the same tongue, same taste for citrus and pâté), but I ordered the whole branzino for myself. It was always known that I would wait, but now—would it break her heart, I asked? The wavering chin. The hard glance away. She could have taken a few more seconds before the *Yes*. I picked at the hem of my birthday dress. It was getting late. Couples migrated to the same side of dark booths. Our waiter asked—her napkin hadn't even made it to her lap—if everything was okay? Her only chance, no steadfast sibling to take the heat. Was I sure? *She* had *me* at forty, and of course it was a change and *yes* the nights were long and bodies start to weigh, to sag regardless. *I think you'll* . . . I wouldn't. Her squid-ink cavatelli began to stink. I wanted to fill myself with something else—hollow-stemmed coupes of champagne, shade-grown coffee, beef tartare alone at noon. We could take that trip to Saint-Tropez! If he did leave, I'd be fine. I looked down into my wine. I need long runs along a country road to keep me sane. As it is, I cannot coax myself to sleep most nights, and we don't even— What I couldn't say: they'd barely get to know her, and dad would be a man we'd tell them lived once. Plus I have so little will most days to stay alive myself. And so she wept. I paid.

The Three Widows

we call them, that week
        at our rented beach shack,
with smiles equally, let's admit,

        tender and cruel.
Heart, cancer, rope—
        they flourished

without men. Designed tiny houses.
        Protested often.
A month in Guatemala.

        Book clubs,
movie groups, wine tasting
        before the play. More friends

than either of us, solitary couple,
        could imagine.
Some old myth unfurling,

        surely, before us
as we haul their bright umbrellas
        down to Great Hollow,

ocean the mouth of that one river
        we all fear.
They're out there in it

        together, bobbing up
and down in the spray,
        giggling like the girls

they insist, each wine-dark evening,
        they once were.
They have each bathed and changed me.

        Made me spit
the sidewalk gum into their palms,
        found me hiding,

after frantic searching, pitched
        threats, on top of the dryer.
Freed from these duties,

        they turn hungry for children,
covet them, on the beach, for hours
        (we don't look up

from our hardbacks)
        as one boy keeps rushing
toward the waves that pummel him.

        "You're not watching!" my mother
thinks to yell at the young, oblivious parents
        who keep turning away.

She looks at me,
        each time he reaches
the water's thinning lip.

        Studied, by now, in pretending
not to notice, I swat a fly.
        My husband turns a page.

Each day we pledge
        more patience (they are not
young) and each day

we fail. So, hungover
from the wine we need
            to stay nice, we consent

to the marsh walk.
            My husband strides ahead.
The widows coo

            into a stroller taking up the trail
and, in the novel
            I can't write until they're all dead,

this is where
            the protagonist (prettier,
more interesting me)

            finally loses her shit,
tells the women how she'd rather
            jump off the bridge and be devoured

by the gathering horseshoe crabs
            than listen to them talk.
("They're bottom-feeders,

            and wouldn't touch you,"
my mother, the scientist,
            would reply in a huff.)

On the real walk I take photographs
            of the three of them
bending toward the child,

            posing against the salt marsh,
pointing at the ancient creatures
            in the estuary below them,

exclaiming to no one
         which one's dead,
which one's living,

         which one's simply shell.

October Moon

It has no title,
my father's photograph.

Orange disk burning
cold in the coal-dark sky.

It has always been October
Moon. When I look up

from my sturdy desk,
when I catch it, turning

a dim corner, this stained orb—
mouth open, swallowing stars.

Why is it this
I see when my husband

tells me I have become
more lovable?

Reader, I

was one of many, in a long ancestral line, one of thousands of women to fuse herself to sorrow. From Napoli, from the strict wooden church of Fürstenberg, his people arrived. From village syntax of sacrifice. From heavy bread. Women who salted the pot with a baby at the breast. Women who strained eyes, peeling their faces, each night, reflected in soft potatoes. *Do you think we deserve happiness?* He asked this often. I had been silly, thinking us special. In imagining some swift departure from women who strapped themselves to their festering elders without a thought. Even in the closest stone huts they left room for an altar. I did not realize I was to become one long cello note, or the short, cold index finger of a German wife. A heroic washing stone. How he longs for ardor, labors to lose himself through eleven-hour days at the desk. Stark Lents. Happiness—ha. So I liked to let bitters fall from a glass dropper into champagne. To take, on occasion, a Wednesday off. He had this motto: work is love. Coarse penance. Rue. Dark centuries of women annihilating my morning walk. All his great-great-grannies unfucking me. So what, my *buon appetito*? Are there moments—the shirked hour of grading, the plucked tulip—that can exist unscathed? What of those giddy nights of dancing in dark clubs? What of Miami's long beach, of mai tais? What of picnics? What of my toe slipped into his mouth?

Adult Swim

Let them eat corn dogs. Let them
peel from its sack a freezer-burnt popsicle,
lime, green as an alien gem.

Let them pluck from the strung garland of chips.

Sugaring their lips with the fine grit
of Sour Patch Kids, these strange children
lift to their mouths those soft little bodies
and chew. They forget, for just a moment, the water
from which they've been banished.
Then a pause in the guard station's country radio—
they pirouette back and begin,
again, to sulk. Gawk.

Let them.

It's nearly time to reclaim
their pool. Each day, each hour
they have dragged their soaking bodies
from its coolness and allowed their mothers
the reapplication of lotion and the petting
of their wet, tender heads.

No agony is greater
than theirs. Never have I felt so powerful.
Aren't I magnificent,
floating on my back dead center? Aren't I
a kingdom of one?
I could grow new gods.
Small princes.

(My grandmother's voice—*if you own nothing
you are nothing*—as she handed me, at Christmas,
a fresh certificate of stock. But she was an unhappy woman,
and is dead.)

A whinny of pain
from a skinned knee, quick flash
of white before the blood. Not my wound
to treat. Another boy explaining to his mother's magazine
how every day, every single day,
God puts out the sun by dunking it in the ocean.
Like a match dropped
into a glass.

Where does the next one come from?
he wants to know.

One up to his thighs already
until the strict whistle, the chorus
of booing beside him,
a leap back.
Lined on the plastic rim, the boys stare differently
than the men they will become.

Where are the wild things?

The boy worries.
Who promises tomorrows to a whole needful planet,
restrikes that match?

Who bears that next fiery sphere?

Who will remind this woman
she's not some queen
acquiring a country estate—ruby brooches, oiled leaves

of topiaries glistening in midday sun—
while the real rural citizens starve. Fountains
upon fountains and a small pond
to reflect back her dais. Crystal plates
of petit fours. For which,
history admonishes, she was beheaded.

ENTR'ACTE

Juliet, From the Balcony

So she says it all, for him to overhear. Narrates her privation.

He's come over the orchard walls. All that rustling through the cypress. Even above the lemon tree blossoms saturating the summer night, she can smell his neck.

She's a minor philosopher, here. Has the semiotic *not* down.

The country-length distance between name and man.

In one painting her pale throat is engulfed, his hand bending her, bending her. In another, two white petals fallen on the balcony steps— minor detail.

There is no balcony.

The playwright has no word for it, 1595.

How badly the audience wants her closer, for her to step from behind the window. Skirt billowing.

See, there is no crest, no marble lip to mount.

When she speaks, she is opera's first monody.

When she speaks, she is the Ponte Pietra above the Adige. Adriatic salt-wind, flesh of hazelnut, milk-just-souring.

Olive groves pulsing before the harvest. Is arbiter of sun and moon.

Bright angel.

When she speaks, she is the amphitheater split *nel mezzo* after the earthquake.

Is the earthquake.

When she speaks she does not say nothing.

V.

Reader, I

had grown skeptical of line. Of stern procession down a page's blue rule. Malmaison's perfumed rows the Empress marched down—*Rosa centifolia, Rosa lucida*—while her husband's flotilla lapped toward Trafalgar. Of the jealous descent. I had cast off such impossible realms— near Diamond Head, on an unseasonably cool August morning, Gloria, great-aunt, finally let go the material world forty minutes after Father was lifted from his last bed. Then I shared the blood of three still-breathings. Lone quatrain, us. Who mostly didn't speak, or write. All to say—when I attended the teeming wedding feasts, the high school graduations from yet another Cleveland cousin, the austere Catholic masses full of *him*, I softened, a bit, my stance. Signed my name inside his family Bible, though I didn't believe. Seventeen casseroles sent postsurgery, reliable piles of Christmas cards. In the frozen cemetery, enough small talk to cancel out a whole, sad self. When I glimpsed, after, the sprawling hand-drawn tree from which he came, I thought of shallow roots. And the women of Greece mourning, each year, mortal Adonis. Reader, some say they were a simple people, who believed in mere symbols, gods of corn. They planted—in the quick, festive flush of summer heat—fennel and barley in terracotta shards. *Gardens of Adonis* they called these small, short-flourishing graves, and when on the eighth day the false flowers withered the women flung them to the sea. Imagine—their dead that present. Listening. So when I make the small cut, insert the orange-flowering Arizona into our disease-resistant, winter-sturdy Wife of Bath, I say a little prayer. *Beautiful, brief Adonis—forgive me my hubris, this dreamy cultivar, this mingled seed.* We wrap grafting tape around the rose's wound. Wife now, I see it. The fresh lesion of two. Tender twinning. We know not what will come after—peach petals, scent of myrrh? A tusked beast rushing from the forest to gut us, four months in hell? But we know what came before. Which ship held which man before he lay down in which new country with which wife. The log they sawed, the plates they stacked. The children they buried and the children that buried them in deep family plots. It astonishes me still how many shared the same name. How his people will gather in the same church gymnasium, in Bucyrus, after the funeral, the baptism, after the wedding for the same creamed chicken. That they stand in the longest lines for that. Reader, I found belief outside belief when for the first time the cicadas weren't screaming, all evening outside our bedroom, *me me me me.*

Hypotactic

Suppose meaning arrives like winter. The scarlet
hawthorn clarified under its crest of snow, a season's
   sentence, refining—what will you keep? What won't you do
for love? Suppose it takes the longest night to see.
   Suppose ice-sealed banks along the Kolyma River
retain not only the campion's whitelace flowers—
   seeds simmering thirty thousand years to bloom again beneath
a Moscow laboratory's false sun—but also a flight of stairs
   revealing the secret bunker where Mussolini held, for the last
time, his pale Claretta; also Hipparchus's vast, observable
   stars. Suppose Gwendolyn Brooks's handwritten recipe
for orange cake floating in permafrost. The first breath
   Eve took, rib-pulled into Eden. *Alongside, alongside.*
Suppose we emerge into ourselves, stepping from the veil
   of a selfish teenage torment that never spins off
early enough to announce to the world, to a father, before
   he vanishes in the next room, *I am not only*
I. Suppose, implied in Greek, in stone, above the temple
   at Delphi, that knowledge requires a journey.
Suppose below the orlop deck the ship carries not only malarial
   chills but girls, tucked behind casks of olive oil, who survived
worse windowless rooms, the nightly. . . . To the creamed
   mixture, fold alternatively dry ingredients and liquids. Suppose
the bottom layer can be crooked if the frosting is thick enough
   to hold. Suppose I'll try the weighted blanket.
A thousand microfiber beads. *Earthing*, some call
   this, cortisol slowed. *Make yourself an offering*
to sleep is what came scripted on the blanket's violet tag.
   Suppose offerings of gold leaf. Sunburnt mirth,
and myrrh. Suppose the new thought the forest clearing
   becomes, appearing light-strung from the over-

growth. Suppose you make an offering of that.

A sublayer of carbon slumber, and Patsy's *tralalalala*,
and a little crumb of madeleine, which will never decompose.

Reader, I

write (perhaps you've noticed) about love. He writes—what a man—of
work. These tired roles. But aren't they mirrors? When in the garden
Eve goes, *Give me a goddamned minute alone in yonder Spring of Roses*
does she a) recite her therapist's decree to give herself a little break
from *we* b) know by now by heart the *Cosmo* clipping on more tasteful
lingerie—*One wants what one can't see*—or c) invent the division of
labor? Adam off winding the woodbine round his wounded ego. But
maybe, keen reader, you long for d) all of the above. That love is work
and work is love and toss me the pruning gloves but I don't want to
see you for at least a day? I've read the Marxist takes—no room for
play makes Adam a dull, bourgie boy. Eve needs to get free, explore
her sexuality with Anja, Ingrid, Jürgen, and Klaus. That sex inside the
marriage house is only ever okay. Or the book that opts completely out,
no future happy ceremony on the statehouse steps, no children getting
in the way. And I agree—*No* is my darling RSVP. But I've always courted
in-between. Tennis with the net down *isn't* any fun, and it takes more
than one to hang the discount Christmas lights. *Frost was right* wasn't
in my wedding letter; when we work alone we love each other better.

Reader, I

learned to love Ohio. Glacial flatlands of his birth. The corner dairy store, the county road where Digger died. I learned how to get a mouth around *Cuyahoga* and *Gallipolis*, the sweet American *I* of *Rio Grande*. I learned to stand for the twilight's last gleaming, for the ramparts we watched, Thursday evenings, at the minor-league stadium. Children collecting the fireworks scraps, postloss, by floodlight. I learned to love their summer nights—that deep damp, hours of storm brightening the clouds. And now that we've left, it's the simmering Rust Belt fight I miss, how it bands around a small-town pitcher, singes the glove. What I love is how he talked there, shearing his *to be*. The Impala that needs washed. How he walked me down small Lake County dunes, through the switchgrass, pale sea rocket, picked the cocklebur from my socks. We would sit in the center of our small side yard, just dusk, tracing the fireflies' big dipper patterns with our eyes. Fall laid us down at the altar of football—I learned all the five-star prospects' names. For high school games we brought a special blanket to drape over the concrete seats: patchwork jerseys from his youth. Truth is, I can celebrate nearly any spectacle with enough cold beer. In Ohio, there was plenty. Coolers upon coolers in his uncle's basement, where I learned thou shalt lead with thy right bower. Even a nonbeliever like me learned to love the explicit rituals of early mass, to let the planted Protect Life signs lie. Lying in a motel bed in Martins Ferry, my husband told me what it means, *Ohio*, what was rushing, rain-swollen, underneath the bridge. *Beautiful river.* Far from clear mountain streams of the West, it took me awhile to see such beauty. Dust-brown deluge, stinking barges of trash. Sometimes you don't have to see straight through a thing. He taught me that. That dirt is merely deliverance from other places.

Reader, I

shit the bed. Postprocedure, the white hospital cot bore my stain. His looking away was barbed with kindness as he strained one of my legs into the sweatpants. Steadied my postfast dance with his palm. Romance? Reader, I'll tell you plainly—it had been five months. The initial glance of *Do you* before the feigned *Perhaps* bled to silence. Pleasure, deduced Mill, was higher as intellect between two. To emancipate the wife would create a dance without a lead, a more fulfilling tête-à-tête. Reigned verbal sparring, reigned equal minds. The senses—atavistic. (There are so many ways a body can betray.) You should know I came out of that anesthetic fog replaying a severe teacher's lines—*In the worst hour of the worst season of the worst year* . . . I wanted a beer. But the machines kept saying my pulse was weak. Three nurses hovered. Beep. Beep. He thought, he told me after, that I was close to being lost. My flesh the color of the cot. He wiped my face. Lingered at my lips to brush a crumb. This was not my worst, he said. He said it like I could be beautiful again. I was so thirsty. The flimsy straw, he held it straight. It wasn't only law, I realized, that held us here, in sickness, in the late light washing us out. It was also the cold dirt, waiting. The nursing home robes. I flashed to us at ninety. And reader? The pain, it dulled.

Reader, I

am sick of *I*. Sole dash. Whining pole. He would never. Is self-less. Is of a stock not so bent on taxonomies of *Me*. Is Ohio-good. Is *work*, is *wait*. Is skilled in weather-talk, in leaving rooms a little in love with him. Is *so handsome, so wise*. Is untouched by the witch of jealousy. Is Olympic-thighed. He sleeps through the entire night. Remembers to wash the car of its winter-salt. He calls his mother. Guffaws at his sister's jokes and makes his Meema's chicken parm. Is little-alarmed. But he cries at the end of sitcoms. Mourns the soul of the trashed mattress, the broken bulb. He loves the RPO, the alma mater. Roots for the backup QB at the bar. Shovels the widow neighbor's drive. At each 11:11, he wishes the same wish. On cold nights he makes dinner pancakes on the griddle, *and* does the sink of dishes. And, when my mother's golden died, he held both paws and told her she was a good dog, a noble dog, until the medicine made her stiff. Then he fixed drinks, got Mom's Manhattan right. When he passes a mirror, dear reader, he hardly ever pauses.

Aphasia

for Mike

"It's so beautiful," you told us
when you could talk again. Pure
sound. Balloon-like, the middle rising.
Name, nearly, of some precocious girl
in Eugene, or mute Greek goddess.
Its origins, though, aren't all disorder—
something of the ineffable, what slips
the tongue in wonder. That which can't
be said. I had been searching
for a happier way to write of love.
Impossible! *All happy families . . .*
All happy poems. *Happy*
isn't what anyone would call you, Mike,
except maybe as an office joke.
I know, now, you like to watch others
approach it. At the Sidney Dairy Barn,
the late-summer cornfields inescapable,
you wanted us so badly to be
content with our chosen fruit flavors.
The lemon some bright home.
Driving us the long way back, past
the farm, past the lone, spotted horse,
past your late wife's favorite church,
you said you could have watched her pray
inside forever. I have finally come to see
how I have relied all my life on the fictions
of long Russian novels and insufferable
grainy films for models of pairing.
That I desired extensive evening speeches

affirming a great beauty I hadn't yet
lost, somber soliloquies of worship,
words as proof. Yesterday I sensed
the room shift. Had the streetlamps
flickered on? Another lightning bug
caught in our antique lamp? No,
Chris was looking at me, from
across the room, while I read. "What?"
I asked. What was it? He shook
his head, smiled. I couldn't say.

EPILOGUE

Lyrical Vows

Human passions, human characters, and human incidents.
—William Wordsworth

Beneath this daytime moon, rising fast above the turnpike, I take you to be more than a point of departure.

Today, I promise you this: to stay in my own lane during each dark tunnel.

Motor oil, pop can scuttling away from a tire. The seatbelt sunburnt across a pale shoulder. Networks of wires rising away from us.

What connects asphalt to the sky, keeps them from tearing?

May we be so industrious. Burn a hole through the ceiling of our love, rendezvous in Paris to make amends.

I travel among unknown men on roads miles above the sea. Little amorists crossing a glacier's dalliance.

You want, I know, to touch them all.

The wild voice in my head. As if that dog could listen to reason.

May we be spontaneous.

I promise kitteny hand jobs from scenic overlooks. The vernal woods below.

O mercy!

I promise to remind you, daily, we will die.

I promise little swooning, much critique. A dubious moral high ground.

A few miles above Breezewood, the FM fizzles.

It's a testament, you said, to how good the song is. How long one endures the static.

May we never be enough.

What stalls time is the overlit trailer hitch. Like an ancient star slid back.

I will regulate my excess.

I will attempt to regulate my excess.

I will be excessive in my attempts.

The trucks screech and grind. The mountain pass screeches and grinds.

Supposedly, the salvation of the entire human race required the apology of a woman.

I promise to be so arrogant. For as long as we shall love.

Coyote open-throated smear.

When I get the courage to leave is when I know I can stay.

No roadside sign says *precipice*.

The difference between potential and dénouement, how one could slip through. How hot the raw core below the highway, our firm belief in the crust.

Every woman knows to bury the man first in her mind.

You, who are terrified of dying.

You, closer than you appear.

I will be brave.

The star-clusters still burn despite the day.

The FM endurable until that turn, that turn, that.

Downhill, the wild mustard, the cows' slow mouths.

The common pleasure of one clear verse.

I promise never to presume us original.

I take you to be.

ACKNOWLEDGMENTS

Adroit Journal: "Reader, I [buried him]"
                                 "Juliet, From the Balcony"
American Poetry Review: "Reader, I [remember the midnights]"
                                 "Reader, I [write (perhaps you've noticed)]"
Beloit Poetry Journal: "Reader, I [*have not so much time for thinking*]"
Bennington Review: "Reader, I [was not, I learned, *dis*interested]"
Blackbird: "American Foursquare"
                                 "The Marriage Plot"
                                 "Hypotactic"
Boston Review: "Reader, I [did take a walk that day]"
                                 "Reader, I [wore the past around my neck]"
                                 "Reader, I [see it first from the window]"
                                 "Reader, I [drank the milk of paradise]"
                                 "Reader, I [am not so hollow-boned]"
Copper Nickel: "Reader, I [made my mother cry]"
Gulf Coast: "Reader, I [swore I'd be a casual bride]"
Iowa Review: "Reader, I [may have been too flip]"
The Journal: "Reader, I [shit the bed]"
Missouri Review: "Mamma V's Basement Lounge"
New England Review: "Reader, I [was, according to Virgil]"
                                 "Her Thoughts on the Hereafter"
                                 "Reader, I [kept my name]"
New Yorker: "GILLY'S BOWL & GRILLE"
                                 "Adult Swim"
Northwest Review: "Aphasia"
Ploughshares: "The Three Widows"
Sewanee Review: "Reader, I [had grown skeptical of line]"
Southeast Review: "Reader, I [fled him like a hind]"
                                 "Reader, I [learned to love Ohio]"
                                 "Reader, I [am sick of *I*]"
Tupelo Quarterly: "Lyrical Vows"
Washington Square Review: "Reader, I [was one of many]"

Thank you, for your support, your time, your encouragement with this book—David Baker, Nicky Beer, Jericho Brown, Brittany Cavallaro, John Drury, Nicholas Friedman, Cate Marvin, Laura Micciche, Jacques Rancourt, Jess Smith, and Jacob Sunderlin. I owe you all a beer, and much more.

Thank you to my family, small but mighty. And thank you to the Kempfs for welcoming me into your big family.

To the wonderful Sarabande team—Kristen Renee Miller, Joanna Englert, Danika Isdahl, Natalie Wollenzien, Sam Hall—you're the absolute best! I feel incredibly lucky to work with all of you. Thank you for your vision, your belief, your care. Thank you, too, to Emma Aprile for the most thoughtful copyedits and to Sarah Flood-Baumann for the fabulous cover design.

And for all your help with these poems, for sharing a life, showing me more, this book is for you, Chris.

photo by Christopher Kempf

Corey Van Landingham is the author of *Antidote* and *Love Letter to Who Owns the Heavens*. A recipient of a National Endowment for the Arts Literature Fellowship and a Wallace Stegner Fellowship from Stanford University, she teaches Creative Writing at the University of Illinois.

Sarabande Books is a nonprofit independent literary press headquartered in Louisville, Kentucky. Established in 1994 to champion poetry, fiction, and essay, we are committed to creating lasting editions that honor exceptional writing. With over two hundred titles in print, we have earned a dedicated readership and a national reputation as a publisher of diverse forms and innovative voices.